CW01637026

Chubb (

Chubb of the Yard, ex-police dog and resident guard at the Highway Inn, is renowned far and wide for his detective skills. However, when the local Police Superintendent chooses to lodge the young Princess Katerina of Glockenstein at the Highway Inn on the last night of her spectacular Royal Tour, it is for another reason. There are rumours of a sinister plot to kidnap the Princess: what more suitable hiding-place than the modest and slightly run-down Highway Inn? But suspicious characters lurk here, too. No one is better-equipped to sniff out trouble than Chubb—even when hampered by a terrible cold. Chubb thus takes it upon himself to protect the Princess, with hilarious results.

Other books by Roy Brown in the Grasshopper series:

The Million Pound Mouse
Shep the Second
Trojan Rides Again
Chubb on the Trail
Chubb to the Rescue

CHUBB CATCHES A COLD

Roy Brown

Illustrated by Margaret Belsky

A Grasshopper Book

Abelard · London

First published 1979 by Abelard-Schuman Limited

ISBN 0 200 72610 2 (Hardback)
ISBN 0 200 72611 0 (Paperback)

Abelard-Schuman Limited
A Member of the Blackie Group
Furnival House, 14/18 High Holborn
London WC1V 6BX
Printed in Great Britain by
Thomson Litho Ltd, East Kilbride, Scotland

I

The Highway Inn was in the grip of winter and the sky had a grubby-grey whiteness as blank as a brooding face.

The trees round the tavern were black skeletons offering ghoulish branches to the half starved birds. The flower beds were a frozen mess and, each morning and night, the car park at the back took on a frosty sheen, the asphalt resembling a scatter of countless cold diamonds.

At the Inn itself, business being less brisk than usual, an air of depression hung about heavier than the leaden sky.

As Barney Stoat, odd job man and bartender, put it, "If it snowed, that would be *something*."

"We're bound to get snow," said Mr Peacock the proprietor.

"We can do without snow," said his daughter Alice.

"Well, there's always Christmas," said Barney.

"Christmas!" said Alice, as if she was referring to some loathsome festival perpetrated by the ancient druids at Stonehenge.

Even at this time of year, Mr Peacock's healthily ruddy complexion managed to light up with optimism, as if sunshine had peeped through a chink in a curtain. "We must count our blessings, Alice. It's cosy and warm inside—you showed considerable foresight, Barney, laying in a good stack of logs. And you must admit, Alice, that having fewer customers to attend to makes your work easier—in the interregnum, so to speak."

"In the *what,* guv?" asked Barney Stoat.

"That is, between now and Christmas. We shall, of course, have our usual family dinner—at a modest charge, to mark the occasion. Let me see, to cheer ourselves up we could begin thinking of decorations. And we still have several excellent young fir trees growing in the wood, one for each of the bars, planted in tastefully adorned tubs, of course."

Barney obstinately shook his head. "If the snow comes the customers will stop at home and watch the telly, unless we supply them with dogs and sledges."

"Good idea, Barney! I think Chubb would rather enjoy being temporarily harnessed to a sleigh—with bells, of course."

"The state he's in," said Barney, "you'd hardly know if he was pulling or pushing."

Alice drew somewhat sinister crosses on the frosty glass of the saloon bar. "This may not be quite the moment to mention it, but in my opinion that old Basset Hound is not long for this world."

"Oh, come off it, Alice," said Barney. "He's only caught a cold."

"And we're keeping an eye on his admittedly rather severe symptoms," nodded Mr Peacock. "Medication three times a day, for instance."

"Yeah," said Barney. "And you don't even have to hold his nose when you tip it down."

Alice snorted. "Since it consists of nine parts best brandy and one part double cream, it's no wonder! Ridiculous extravagance—it's disgusting how that old dog sneezes on the floor and coughs on the carpets. Most unhygienic! And his temper . . . no one could ever call Chubb an amiable beast at the best of times, but since he caught this cold as you call it, though personally I would say it was something far *worse*, I'm terrified to go near him. Yesterday, for instance, he was in the lounge bar while I was cleaning. I was lucky to get out of the room with all four limbs intact."

Barney said, "It's that fancy new mop of yours, Alice. Chubb is probably allergic to goose feathers and even more allergic to being poked in the ear and shooed off his favourite mat at the end of a six foot cane."

"I do see your problem, Alice," said Mr Peacock in his usual placatory way. "When one is a little off colour it is best not to be a nuisance, particularly within the bosom of one's family. I'll have a word

with him about it."

"You'll do *what,* guv?" asked Barney.

"That is to say..." stammered Mr Peacock in some confusion. "Suppose we made him up a bed in the wine cellar?"

"The wine cellar!" said Alice. "Last time Chubb was down there he discovered a leaky barrel of best cognac. For a week he was reeling about all over the place, completely out of his senses. If there's one thing worse than a Basset Hound with a cold, it's a tipsy old dog who leers at the customers."

"Yes, well... we'd all better find something to occupy our hands. No use letting the weather cast its shadow. *Nihil desperandum,* so to speak. Barney, we could do with some more logs from the wood before the snow actually arrives. And, Alice, I wonder if you could find the time to clean the silver? One never knows, we might suddenly have a coach party wanting a five course dinner."

"That's a laugh," said Barney, his expression anything but hilarious. "Coaches never come here in winter. Nothing *never* happens to us, in winter. Still, the daily round, the common task, as the man said. I'll just pop up and fetch me mittens. Axe is a bit blunt, though. Even the trees is frozen stiff."

That evening, as was his custom, Chubb joined Mr Peacock in the snuggery, nestling among the cushions in what had once been the retired policeman's favourite chair.

On these occasions, Mr Peacock habitually played a record on his hi-fi set. This was not only because Chubb had an ear for music, but also because the sonorous chords would conceal, from anyone indiscreet or inquisitive enough to listen beyond the door, the fact that conversations of an extraordinary nature regularly took place within.

It had always been the Basset Hound's custom, throughout a long and distinguished career as a detective dog at Scotland Yard, to appoint his immediate superior officer as sole human confidant—a privilege which nowadays, during his period of semi-retirement, he thought suitable to bestow upon an ex-Inspector of the Kent Constabulary.

Chubb sprawled amidst the cushions in a somewhat sorry stance, large nose hot and dry, breath coming in starts and stops, eyes dulled over and perceptibly out of focus.

Mr Peacock carefully selected a record from his collection. He hastily rejected a funeral march to which he happened to be attached, dismissed, without hesitation, his favourite Requiem Mass, and eventually alighted upon a cheerful but soothing rendering of the Sugar Plum Fairy.

Chubb's response, however, was to close his eyes, screw up every muscle in his immense, shivering body and succumb to a tremulous and terrible spasm of coughing which racked the room.

Mr Peacock waited for the convulsions to die down before sadly shaking his head and saying, "I'm afraid you're not in very good shape, old fellow."

"A cold," said Chubb, choking on the words. "A mere cold, Inspector. Nothing, I assure you. But a condition worsened, I fear, by being denied access to the saloon bar fire last night. And all over a sneeze—a sneeze, Inspector! Furthermore—and here I may add that, as you know, I am not given to undue complaint—being assaulted with a feather mop does little to alleviate an old dog's afflictions. A-tishoo!"

Mr Peacock waited for the chair to cease rocking. "Quite wretched. I wonder, however, whether we might, if at all possible, avoid sneezing on our velvet cushions? An old newspaper, perhaps..."

Chubb opened one bleary eye. "A sneeze is a sneeze, Inspector. It comes when it comes. It goes when it goes. Placing my head on a dusty old newspaper would scarcely help. Ah, Inspector, if winter is here, can spring be far behind?"

"A fair distance, I should say," observed Mr Peacock. "We have Christmas to get through, yet. As I was saying to Alice..."

Chubb did not appear inclined to discuss Alice. His next words had a nasal twang, not because he was a dog but because the passages of his large nose were utterly blocked. "It was nearing Christmas, Inspector, long ago, when I caught my last cold."

"Fancy! While you were still at the Yard, presumably."

"Naturally—where else?" said Chubb, closing his eye again. (Not merely because his tear ducts were congested but because when you looked at the past, it was better not to have too clear a view of the present.) "I have previously mentioned my Dicken Medal, Inspector?"

"Yes, to be sure you have!"

"And Bar."

"And Bar, of course."

"The river was half frozen, Inspector. A child had slipped from a barge and fallen clean through a hole in the ice. I happened to be on the scene at the time. Duty, naturally—the Case of the Deptford Drifters, I believe. Or was it that spot of bother we had with the smuggler, Jettison Jack? Never mind ... the fact remains that I plunged in at once, drilling a second hole in the ice. Quite a simple stratagem, Inspector,

to a resourceful young detective dog in his prime."

"Great Scot!" exclaimed Mr Peacock. "You might easily have both been lost, Chubb, if you had, from under the surface, failed to locate one of the holes in the ice."

Chubb struggled to continue between coughs. "Merely a matter of blasting a *third* hole, Inspector. With my nose, of course."

"Excellent, old chap!"

Chubb flicked his tail. "Unseemly, Inspector, to make too much of one's youthful prowess. Who am I to boast? All one may, perhaps, point out is that one does not obtain the Dicken Medal and Bar as a free gift in a packet of dog biscuits! I remember, after this trifling incident, Commander Crime at the Yard being most sympathetic. I inadvertently sneezed on his carpet, I recall, and he patted my head and said, 'Poor Chubb! Don't be in the least put out. Sneezes come and sneezes go. Here, jump up and do it right here on my desk if you wish.' Which goes to show, Inspector, that there are differing opinions as to sneezes. A-tishoo!"

On this occasion Mr Peacock desisted from comment. "Look here, old chap, I have been thinking . . . it doesn't do to neglect a cold. Why not have the veterinary surgeon call? Old Mr Whelp, I understand, is in the district at the moment. Attending Lady Chatterton's cats, you know. I'm sure he'd feel honoured to spare an hour to pop by and give us the benefit of his medical expertise."

For some reason Chubb was not immediately enthusiastic. "Ah, vets, Inspector. Excellent fellows, vets. For well bred cats—quite indispensive. Also, I believe, not entirely unexpeditious with sick cows and sheep. As to dogs, however—dogs of a certain breeding, one has to be more cautious. In short, veterinary persons have a regrettable habit of administering treatments. Castor oil for instance—ruinous to one's digestion. And pneumatics, even worse."

"Pardon?"

"Pneumatics, Inspector, which taste abominably and, on the whole, have a most grievous effect."

"Oh, you mean *emetics*."

"Precisely, Inspector. Emetics is what I said." Chubb produced a third sneeze into the nearest cushion. He went on, "I would prefer to continue, for the moment, to place myself entirely in your good hands, Inspector. I rather think, by the way, it is time for my medicine."

Mr Peacock glanced at his watch. "Good gracious, you're quite right! I'll fetch it at once."

Chubb snuffled and choked. "How I shall manage, for the third time today, to swallow the mixture you force into my swollen throat I cannot tell. However, Inspector, in the circumstances one must be, shall we say, ruthless—strike at the heart of the malady without compunctiousness. Shall we say, two measures of brandy—and, perhaps, just a *little* extra dash of double cream?"

2

A day or so later a police car slithered to a standstill in the frosty car park behind the Inn, blue light twinkling.

Out climbed no less a personage than the local Superintendent of Police, cautiously negotiating the slippery path in his big boots and long legs and eventually finding Mr Peacock alone in his study, at work on his memoirs.

"Ah, Superintendent," said Mr Peacock. "It's some time since we were favoured with a visit from you."

"Yes . . . mustn't stay long. Snow's on the way. Five miles from here it's already a foot deep and we're having problems supervising the traffic trying to cross the bridge. Never mind that . . . I have a piece of news, Inspector, that will astound you, I'm sure."

Mr Peacock smiled wryly, knowing full well that when the Superintendent addressed him by his former rank it meant that he, Mr Peacock, was about to be persuaded, however unwillingly, to help out with certain police activities during which the Superintendent would establish his seniority. Not, he hoped, being dragged off in his Landrover to set up a road block at the snowed up bridge.

However, on this occasion, the Superintendent merely twitched his large moustache, placed his peaked cap on Mr Peacock's desk and said, positively beaming, "Tell me, Inspector, how do you fancy a visit from Royalty?"

"Good gracious," gasped Mr Peacock.

"I thought that would make you sit up! Rather a complicated story which I will keep as short as possible. You've heard, of course, of a country called Glockenstein?"

"Glockenstein? Now let me think . . ."

"No time for that! Let me refresh your memory. Glockenstein is one of the last remaining independent principalities in Europe. Royal. King Hugo, you know."

"Ah, of course," said Mr Peacock, vaguely. "Glockenstein. King Hugo. Yes, yes."

"Quite," nodded the Superintendent. "Now suppose I was to tell you that his only daughter, heiress to the throne, has been making a goodwill tour of this country. Must have read about it in the papers, surely, Inspector. I refer, of course, to the Princess Katerina of Glockenstein. Still very young and, strictly between ourselves, something of a headache to the police authorities." He lowered his voice, as if the enemies of the state of Glockenstein might already have planted a microphone on the wall of Mr Peacock's snuggery. "We have wind of a plot, Inspector—an invidious scheme to abduct the Princess and hold her to ransom. Terrorists will stop at nothing . . . nothing. Of course, she is heavily guarded. Her entourage, you know. Chaperone, chauffeur, bodyguard—even a dog, I understand, which they keep underfed and in a perpetually ugly mood. A Dobermann, in fact—nothing more ferocious ever strutted the earth."

"Er—so I believe," nodded Mr Peacock. "You said something about headaches, Superintendent?"

"Ah, well. The Princess Katerina is a wilful young lady. Likes her own way, and all that. Hasn't in the least enjoyed being watched over and guarded night and day. Rather naughty at garden parties, I gather, and do you know what the young madam once did? Disappeared for a night and was found next morning, filthy as an urchin, tunnelling her way through a twenty-foot pipe in an adventure playground in Hackney! Had the Home Office hopping like frogs."

"I can well understand it."

"Dog recovered her. The Dobermann, Heinz—after the beans, you know. Talking of dogs, Inspector... do you still own a dog?"

"My Basset Hound, Chubb."

"I remember him well!"

"He's rather poorly at present."

"I wondered why he wasn't lying on the floor like a mat, waiting to be trodden on! A matter of detail, Inspector. I'm afraid something will have to be done about him. We hardly need a sensational item in the local newspaper about a decrepit old Basset Hound being mauled to death by Princess Katerina's Dobermann, do we? Never mind, for the moment. The point is, the higher ups require somewhere en route where the Princess and her entourage can stay overnight before catching their Royal Yacht moored at Dover. Due to sail in a few days' time—depends on the weather forecast. The party will reach us tomorrow night—meanwhile I shall have to move some men in to tighten up the security arrangements. Any problems, Inspector?"

"None at all."

"Excellent! I'm sure you'll be equal to the occasion. You have sufficient accommodation, I believe? The entourage will be arriving in their car—Mercedes, of course. No flag on the front. Last thing we want, Inspector, is to draw attention to their presence. The terrorists could be anywhere—anywhere."

"Perfectly understood, Superintendent. May I say, this is something of an honour."

"Quite." The Superintendent gave his moustache a satisfied twirl. "It simply happened that the Authorities required some hostelry off the Dover road. Obscure, unnoticeable, nondescript, not particularly distinguished. After all, with things as they are—and especially bearing in mind the Princess Katerina's—er—wanderlust, a five star hotel would, at this stage, attract far too much attention."

Mr Peacock turned slightly pink. "Actually, Superintendent, we do have *one* star you know!"

"I dare say," observed the Superintendent, not over impressed. "I count on you, Inspector, to use the utmost discretion. No chit-chat in the bar. And tell your staff only the barest facts. By the way, we shall be erecting an emergency fence."

"Fence?"

"Yes, a rush job, of course. But extra precautions are called for, don't you think? Electric. Two thousand volts will be enough—we'll bring in a special generator. And remember, no dog on the premises. Chain him up somewhere out of sight. In his own best interests, of course! Have you seen what a Dobermann can do, Inspector, especially when he's kept short of meat? There was a case in Pimlico during the Royal visit, I remember. Guardsman on a horse, St James's Palace. Heinz took it into his head to attack. Those guardsmen are not there just to look pretty for the tourists, you know. Fellow drew his sword, Heinz snatched it out of his hand. Almost a serious diplomatic incident . . ."

When Mr Peacock broke the news, Alice bit her lip as if the Highway Inn was about to be taken over by a bunch of Lithuanian refugees with snow on their boots. "This is rather sudden, isn't it? How am I to get the bedrooms ready in time? The saloon bar needs new wallpaper. That dreadful coach party in August, from Islington or somewhere, let their children pick at the pattern with their fingernails."

But Barney Stoat's innocent, boyish face was full of smiles. "Cor! Royalty, eh? Does that mean we shove a flag up on the roof, guv? I'll have to take a peek at my weekly encyclopaedia and find out what colours they fly in Glockenstein. Or will the Union Jack do?"

Mr Peacock shook his head patiently. "That is the point I was trying to make, Barney. The Princess is travelling incognito . . ."

"Yeah, well you wouldn't expect her to do it on horseback!"

"No, no, Barney. Incognito means *secret*. No brass bands. No flag on the Mercedes. No fuss. Remember, the little Princess may be in danger. International intrigue, you know. Probably something to do with the European Economic Community—most things are. You see Barney, the party have had an exhausting schedule. They might have done the journey to Dover in one go, but, according to the Superintendent, it was thought wise to give them one night's break on the way. The Authorities, the Home Office, MI6 and so on, chose us for the honour of entertaining them, presumably because we are not without reputation in the County. It was desirable, of course, that the Princess and her entourage should enjoy all the amenities of the Ritz Hotel without the ostentation which, unfortunately, attaches to such establishments. We are, as you know, starred in the various directories."

"Yeah," nodded Barney. "We just made it if you remember, guv, because we promised the bloke from the AA we'd unblock the drain on the east side. Anyway, one thing's for sure."

"What's that, Barney?"

"We'll have to find a red carpet, won't we? Come to think, there's a spare strip down in the wine cellar. The bit we ripped up from the back passage before the RAC Inspector pitched up. If Alice gives it a good run over with the Hoover, it'll look as good as new."

"I think not, Barney," said Mr Peacock. "A red

carpet could be seen rather easily from the air, don't you think? Now, the Superintendent has obtained my permission to make certain other arrangements. For instance, we are to be fenced in. The wire is to be electrified—worth mentioning in case either of you thought of taking your usual short cut into the village. It'll only be for a few hours and I dare say the police will provide a gate."

"Blimey, with a machine gun post and all?"

Mr Peacock coughed. "There is one other delicate matter I should mention. It concerns Chubb. For the moment, I would prefer that you didn't betray anything in your manner to suggest that special events are afoot—especially since his cold has made him a little touchy of late. The point is, the Superintendent insists that Chubb be given suitable quarters outside the building. As a matter of fact, I happened to notice an excellent kennel at the carpenter's this morning. Mind you, I'm not at all sure how Chubb will take to a kennel, but it can't be helped."

Alice sniffed. "I can't say that I care for our Superintendent but I must admit there are times when he shows considerable sense! How soon do we get the kennel?"

"We already have it! In the back of the wagon. You'd better give me a hand with it later, Barney. Good gracious," he added, peering through the misty windows. "The police are on their toes. Two vans full, just arrived."

Barney Stoat stared through the window. "All they want is a squadron of tanks and we'll be ready for World War Three! Well, I'd best get cracking, and all. Before they shove that fence up, I'm nipping down to the library."

"Really, Barney," frowned Mr Peacock. "Surely this is hardly the time to take up serious reading?"

"Not reading, guv. Cookery. If we've got Royalty coming to stay, I can hardly dish up baked beans on toast, can I? I wonder, when they have a good nosh up in Glockenstein, what they stick their teeth into? Anyway, in the kitchen I'm going Continental!"

3

Mr Peacock was not looking forward to his impending interview with Chubb. Early that evening, unsure how to broach the subject, he sat watching the Basset Hound for some time, wondering if—indeed, half hoping—he had entered a coma (temporary and harmless, of course) so that matters could be held over till a more propitious time.

The Basset Hound's ungainly body was sprawled at an impossible angle in the chair and for alarming periods he stopped breathing altogether. Then sounds emerged from his huge, pink mouth resembling the scrape of emery paper on rusty iron.

Finally one eye opened and Mr Peacock braced himself for the inevitable. "Well, old chap, how is the cold?"

"Grumph!" said Chubb, which was the only sign that the old dog's ears had so far escaped the awful affliction which had reduced the rest of him to an inert and shivering mass.

"What you need, old fellow, is a little piece of news to cheer you up. It can scarcely have escaped your notice that an unprecedented degree of activity is taking place around the Inn."

On second thoughts, Mr Peacock decided that some such oversight was possible. Chubb's eyelids were mostly gummed tightly together and his normally sensitive, exquisitely trained nose was somewhat out of tune. Besides, Mr Peacock had reason to believe that Chubb had spent most of the day slumbering feverishly in Alice's broom cupboard.

"In short," continued the retired Inspector, "we are about to be honoured with a visit from Royalty. What d'you think of that, eh?"

For some reason the announcement failed to have quite the galvanising effect on the Basset Hound which Mr Peacock had expected. Chubb sneezed, just the once, and forced one eye open. "Ah! Not altogether an astonishment, Inspector. Not an *astonishment*, one might say. The Duke, perhaps. Possibly even Her Majesty in person?"

"Actually it's the Princess K—"

"Ah, of course, the Princess. News travels fast, Inspector. So kind, that Her Royal Highness should hear of my infirmity and take the trouble to call and offer her condolences. We were once acquainted, you know."

"But look here, old chap..."

"I must have referred, at some time, to what

occurred at the Garden Party?"

"Garden Party . . . where was that, old chap?"

"Buckingham Palace, of course. Where else? If one says *Garden Party,* Inspector, one can only be referring to Buckingham Palace. I was assigned there as Guard Dog. Special Branch, you know. And there was the almost calamitous affair over the Cream Cakes."

"Cream cakes!"

Chubb closed the first eye again and wrenched open the second. "While we have the opportunity, Inspector, we might jot down a note or two. For the memoirs, of course."

"Of course!" Mr Peacock found his pen and wrote CREAM CAKES, not sorry to have an excuse to put off, however briefly, the subject uppermost in his mind.

"Not *ordinary* cream cakes, Inspector," growled Chubb. "Ordinary is not what they were."

Mr Peacock patiently wrote: EXTRAORDINARY CREAM CAKES.

"The cakes," went on the Basset Hound, his voice hoarse, but otherwise recovering a spark of his former vitality and alertness, "had about them a certain suspiciousness. There were villains afoot, Inspector, for all that they wore top hats and tails, whose purpose, as Special Branch had made clear, was to tamper maliciously with the cream cakes. I well remember the Commissioner himself presiding at the briefing conference—sealed room at the Yard, you know. He said, as I recall, 'If there is some possibility that the cream cakes are not all they should be, then this is a case for Chubb. Chubb will sniff out the truth!' I trust I am not boring you, Inspector?"

"No, but . . ."

"I will pass over the day's events as swiftly as I can. For instance, it would be tedious to mention that on my way through the gates of Buckingham Palace I was privileged to apprehend two pick pockets. But, as I say, my chief assignment was of far greater historical validitude. I moved freely about, incognito as always, amongst the mightiest of the land. Dignitaries, potentates, even, if my memory serves me, the President of the United States. No, that would have been the following year—when I was assigned to that most tanglous case of the Court Butcher and his mislaid meat axe.

"But as to the cakes, Inspector," sneezed Chubb. "There were several platefuls on the Royal table itself. The Princess in particular, as I well knew, was extremely partial to cream cakes—and there she was, taking one in her dainty hand. One bite, I thought, and we might all be plunged at once into national mourning. Ah, Inspector, as I'm sure you know from your own modest but worthy career as a policeman, there are times to ACT. ACT, Inspector, with no thought for life or limb. In short, I *launched* myself at the Royal table and sent the odious cakes scattering. 'Begging your pardon, Your Royal

Highness,' I managed to blurt out as I knocked the Princess off her feet—a simple stratagem, of course, to ensure that the poison never reached her lips."

"Excellent!" gasped Mr Peacock, glancing at his watch. "But what happened to the scattered cakes?"

"Consumed," said Chubb, drawing a pink, parched tongue across his mouth, as if in some private and not unpleasant recollection. "After all, Inspector, a detective dog unprepared to lay down his digestion, or even life itself, in defence of his Royal betters, is, so to speak, scarcely worth the onion."

"So the cakes weren't poisoned after all!"

"My dear Inspector, would I be here enjoying your humble amenities if it were otherwise? But one must, of course, take the wheel for the reed . . ."

"I rather think, old chap, you mean *the will for the deed*."

"Precisely! At any rate, my heroism did not go unappreciated."

"I'm sure it didn't."

"The Duke, I remember, patted me and said, 'Well done, Chubb. We shall not forget.' Then Her Majesty came by and tickled my chin. I was of an age when gestures of affection and gratitude are somewhat more frequent than in one's later years: 'Chubb, you fine fellow, we are at a loss how to repay you. A knighthood would be most inadequate, the Royal Garter itself little more than an insult.' Or words to that effect. It would have been unseemly to have replied. One is after all, a dog. I merely bowed my head, licked Her Majesty's hand, then departed about my further duties. There were some sausage rolls, Inspector, which had also about them a taint of suspiciousness . . ."

"Ahem!" said Mr Peacock. "By the way, it is remarkable that you should mention a princess . . ."

Chubb sneezed, nodded, then scratched one suffering ear with a long claw. "Say no more, Inspector. I dare say you, too, are not ungratified that the Princess has demeaned herself to stay, regardless of privation, at a one-star hotel . . ."

Mr Peacock turned pink for the second time that day. "If only you'd let me finish, old chap! I was about to point out that *this* Princess is quite another. She is heiress to the throne of Glockenstein."

Chubb was not in the least put out. "Ah, Inspector, Glockenstein. I know it well. A special team from Scotland Yard was once invited to visit that beautiful little country, to advise on Police methods, you know. At the time, all they had to keep law and order was a man and a boy in a feather hat carrying a pitchfork. I had the privilege of accompanying the mission. Surely I must have told you of the Case of the Sour Sauerkraut?"

Mr Peacock's patience was now entirely exhausted. "Chubb, old chap, do let us concentrate on the young Princess Katerina. She is staying overnight on her way to Dover, with a small entourage. The Authorities are most insistent that no stone be left unturned to protect her from villains who may be planning to abduct her—Reasons of State, you know. Naturally, I've promised to co-operate to the full with our Superintendent."

"Grumph!" said Chubb.

"Yes, I know you haven't always seen eye to eye, but this is a case where one must put duty above personal feelings. I've made it clear to the Superintendent that, with your long and illustrious career at Scotland Yard, you will have a key position." Mr Peacock sharpened his voice with the incisive tone of a Senior Police Officer, "Now, it is quite clear, Chubb, that coughing and spluttering about the hotel would not really make full use of your gifts. You may, of course feel that your present poor health renders such duties impossible, but should you agree, old fellow, to do your best, the Superintendent and I—and also, one may say, the entire Western World—would be most grateful."

Mr Peacock thought it safe to assume that the noises emanating from the Basset Hound's throat were not entirely deprecatory to the idea in principle, so he hastened on: "Our idea is that you should be placed in the proximity of the hotel, with every facility and comfort, in charge of an Advanced Observation Post. Out there, those clear eyes and that marvellous nose of yours will be of inestimable value—*inestimable*, Chubb. What do you say?"

Chubb lurched from one side to the other and stifled a further sneeze. "Naturally, Inspector, as always I am at the disposal of the Kent Con-

stabulary. Out *there,* you said, Inspector?"

"Not exactly *out,* old chap."

"Ah, I see. Yes, yes. An Observation Post... adequately equipped, with full surveillance of the Inn and its environs. I do believe, Inspector, that I know just the place you have in mind. Lady Chatterton's little lodge, perhaps? Well stocked, I remember, even at this time of year, with preserves and, I recall, a small but sufficient cellar where a winter sojourner may occasionally take a little liquid refreshment for medicinal purposes."

"I'm afraid..." said Mr Peacock.

With remarkably little effort Chubb half got out of

his chair, as if he were about to lick Mr Peacock's hand. "No need to apologise, I assure you, Inspector. I am prepared to move to my new quarters at once."

"Actually—um . . ." began Mr Peacock in some discomfiture. "I don't think Lady Chatterton's lodge would be *quite* suitable to our purpose. Rather an *obvious* landmark, I should say. We—er—that is to say I—er—thought of a kennel-type building."

Chubb returned stiffly but hastily to his chair. "I'm afraid my hearing is somewhat impaired, Inspector. Grmph! For a second, I was sure you used the word *kennel*."

Mr Peacock laughed uneasily. "Now look here, old chap, there are kennels and *kennels*. Don't imagine that we would ask you, even in the line of duty, to rough it or anything of that sort. This is a very special kennel. Camouflaged, naturally. Perfect strategic position. And at this very moment Barney is lining it with spare feather mattresses and we are hoping to persuade Alice to part with her own electric blanket for a night or two. There are windows—glass of course, and a door which, with a little practice, you can open and shut at will. Now, if you're not too tired and off colour, old chap, I think before it grows too dark you might care to inspect the premises and see if everything meets with your satisfaction."

In the silence which ensued Chubb sneezed twice then shivered and said, "Very well, Inspector. In the circumstances, of course, I must bow to your superior judgement. If you say kennel, then kennel it must be. Feather mattresses, or beds of nails. Windows, you said? I trust the view of that absurd wire fence the local police are erecting will bring solace to an old dog's eyes! As for the door you referred to, I doubt whether you, in your haste, will have given a moment's thought to the fact that doors are draughts. Open or shut, Inspector—*draughts*, are what doors are. I take it I may have just a few last moments amongst your cushions to prepare myself for the ordeal ahead?"

"Oh, certainly, old chap," sighed Mr Peacock, with some relief. "Take all the time in the world. And may I, on behalf of the Forces of Law and Order, in this country and abroad—not to mention the newly trained police organisation of Glockenstein itself—thank you for the most reasonable and good natured way in which, with no word of demur, you have undertaken this most exacting new assignment?"

4

It was with some ceremony that Mr Peacock, Alice and Barney accompanied Chubb to his new abode. Mr Peacock, who had often pointed out that Chubb was quick on the uptake, described the kennel in a loud voice as "FIELD HEADQUARTERS, TACTICAL COMMAND."

Barney had previously furnished the kennel with a soft mattress and was encountering only a temporary hitch with the central heating. He announced as loudly as possible, "JUST A MATTER OF CONNECTING ALICE'S ELECTRIC BLANKET TO A PLUG IN THE KITCHEN, GUV. COR, I WOULDN'T MIND A KIP DOWN HERE MYSELF. SNUG, ISN'T IT?"

Alice was quite excited. "WHAT A DEAR LITTLE DOOR! WINDOWS, TOO. IF I GET A SPARE MOMENT, I'LL MAKE HIM SOME CURTAINS."

"VERY THOUGHTFUL OF YOU ALICE!"

shouted Mr Peacock. "I THINK, BARNEY, CHUBB MIGHT HAVE A SECOND SUPPER TONIGHT—JUST TO HELP SETTLE HIM IN."

"GLAD YOU MENTIONED THAT, GUV," roared Barney. "I'M WORKING ON IT. HOW ABOUT SCHINKENCREMEROULADE? HAM ROLL TO YOU, GUV." With commendable enthusiasm Barney had swiftly absorbed the recipes in his borrowed cookery books and was even having a fair crack at the pronunciations. "AND TO ROUND OFF WITH, BISKOTTEN AUFLAUF—SPONGE FINGERS TO YOU, ALICE, COOKED IN WINE!"

They stooped down and gazed hopefully through the little trap door. Chubb lay in a somewhat twisted position—the kennel had probably not yet been designed that would house, with entire satisfaction, a Basset Hound of such generous proportions.

Chubb's nose rested on his forepaws and he seemed to have dropped off to sleep already—except that one sickly eye glared at them through the door with a mixture of suspicion, resentment, long-suffering disdain, and other emotions less easy to discern.

Mr Peacock said, "DON'T FORGET, OLD CHAP, HOW TO WORK THE DOOR, SPECIALLY DESIGNED, YOU KNOW, FOR DOGS OF SUPERIOR INTELLIGENCE."

Chubb sneezed through it. Alice giggled. "I never

thought we'd see the day. Chubb, actually in a kennel! No chain?"

"Certainly not!" exclaimed Mr Peacock, horrified.

"Not even a collar?"

"Really, Alice. Unthinkable!"

Although, so far, the preparations for the reception of the Royal Party had not gone at all amiss, Mr Peacock spent a restless and uneasy night. Whether he closed his eyes or opened them, that last glimpse of the Basset Hound's pensive stare through the kennel door haunted him like an apparition.

In the circumstances a nightmare was inevitable—something to do with Barney getting his wires mixed up and connecting Alice's blanket to the Superintendent's generator. Two thousand volts, no less, crackling through the indolent and defenceless Chubb! Then Barney sidling into Mr Peacock's bedroom, steaming plate in hand: "Grub up, guv. Grieze Widenestrachen Baskhund—Hot Dog, to you, fried in castor oil!"

In the next room, under the eaves, Alice also passed a fitful and frozen night, bereft of her electric blanket. And in yet another room Barney Stoat got up, once, to slam his window shut. Then he spent a sleepless hour or more wondering what to serve for breakfast. Pfifferlingsalat?—pickled mushrooms to you, mate. Blimey, these Glockensteinians must have tummies lined with asbestos!

Mr Peacock rose early, put on his fur-lined jacket, crept downstairs and ventured out in the direction of Chubb's kennel.

Either Chubb had, after all, taken the trouble to close his door, or the wind had slammed it shut. Mr Peacock approached with due caution, feet crunching in the white frost. With respectful and funereal progress, as if the kennel might already be a tomb, he steeled himself, bent down and opened the door.

Chubb presented one wakeful if bleary eye which, although reassuring in one sense, in another sent an extra shiver down Mr Peacock's spine. "Hello, old chap. Had a comfortable night?"

"Grumph!" said Chubb, sneezing and coughing in turn. "On the whole, Inspector, and taking everything into account, I console myself that fate could be worse. Worse, Inspector. One should be grateful, perhaps. No doubt there are dogs in a more grievous plight. Mongrels in the streets, for instance, with only dustbins behind which to shelter. Dogs pulling sledges in polar regions. Curs tied to posts, feeding on scraps, even nearer desolation and starvation than myself, waiting for some kindly dustman to throw a mouldy bone from his cart."

"Well, yes, old chap," said Mr Peacock. "Breakfast won't be long. How's the appetite this morning?"

"Poorly, Inspector," said Chubb choking on the words. "In short, poorly is what it is. I have had a change of mind."

"About what, old fellow?"

"During the long wakeful night, Inspector, with the wind beating on my hutch—I must add that the experience gives one some insight into how a rabbit must feel—it occurred to me that a little medical attention might be desirable. You mentioned a vet . . ."

"Ah, so I did," said Mr Peacock. "Certainly, old chap. You would like the vet to call?"

By now Chubb's nose was so far out of the kennel door that there was frost forming on his already grey whiskers. "Not *like,* Inspector. *Like* is not quite the word I would use. Necessity, perhaps. It is probably already too late. However, it might be a revelation were a properly qualified person to witness my present predicament. Possibly he will have advice to offer, especially with regard to the suitability of the habitat—even bearing in mind the oneracious duties laid upon me—in which an old dog should pass the twilight of his years."

"Are you saying, old chap, that you are not perfectly comfortable and content where you are? Very well, if you feel so strongly . . ."

"Not *strongly,* Inspector," said Chubb, the words immediately lost in a fresh bout of throaty sneezing. "*Weakly,* might be a more appropriate word."

"Then I shall telephone the vet at once. Just you snuggle up nice and warm—and don't go away. I'll close your door to keep out the cold." But by the time Mr Peacock had bent down the door had already mysteriously snapped shut.

Within the hour old Mr Whelp clattered into the car park in his ancient vehicle, attired in tweeds and a deerstalker hat.

He brought his bag to Chubb's kennel, crawled through the opening and gave the Basset Hound a thorough examination: pokings with his stethoscope, for instance, and proddings with an instrument resembling a Japanese stiletto.

"Ah!" he snorted wisely, crawling out again. "*Virus Caninculus.*" He wiped a dew drop from his nose and launched into discourse. "At first I thought it was Tinker's Tail Disease. Lot of that about, just now. Then it occurred to me that the poor old fellow might be suffering from *Distemperus Basseticus.* Fortunately not—definitely *not Distemperus Basseticus.* Breathing rather alarming however. Overweight, of course. Insufficient exercise, perhaps?"

"Well . . ."

"Over feeding?"

"Um . . ."

"Tut, tut! Snacks in the bar, eh? Personally I am rather against snacks. Plain, wholesome food, Mr Peacock . . . one tin per day. As I'm sure you've noticed in the TV advertisements, there are many suitable brands. And water, of course—clean water to drink. I rather fancy, from a cursory examination, I confess, that his liquid intake appears to have been contaminated by something rather reminiscent of alcohol! Absurd, of course—probably only his breath. *Virus Caninculus* sometimes has that effect... and he should be kept reasonably warm, Mr Peacock. Warmth, but, at the same time, fresh air in abundance."

Mr Peacock brightened, temporarily overlooking his perhaps over-zealous co-operation with the Kent police. "Ah! So your advice is that Chubb be moved back indoors? My little snuggery, perhaps, with the windows open?"

Mr Whelp was horrified. "Certainly not! His coat, you know. Alarmingly thin—quite bald in patches. Comes from too much central heating and log fires. Bad for the teeth too. This is an excellent kennel, Mr Peacock. Excellent! I should leave the door open at all times. Let the good, clean air rush in, *rush in,* at will. Do wonders for his coat out here! The old dog still has a certain amount of natural body heat. *Virus Caninculus,* you know, needs to be *frozen* out. However, I will leave you a prescription... he may object to the taste at first. I suggest holding his nose... now what *did* I do with the other half of my stethoscope?"

When the vet had driven off, Mr Peacock tiptoed through the heavy frost towards Chubb's kennel. He crunched half way there then, on second thoughts, crunched the half way back, slipped into the Inn unseen and went in search of the dependable Barney Stoat.

Common sense, in Mr Peacock's experience, often did much to temper medical mumbo jumbo. And fresh air, he thought, as he coughed his way through the Inn door, was all very well in its place—preferably in some Siberian forest where nobody but a few hardy Russian peasants could feel it.

As for medicine, Mr Peacock did not relish trying to force a giant spoon into the Basset Hound's reluctant mouth, perhaps having to borrow a couple of burly coppers to sit on Chubb's rear quarters whilst the dose was administered.

Barney was in his apron and cap. There was a distinct lack of the usual fragrant and familiar odour of sizzling bacon and eggs spluttering in pans. Barney was using a chopping knife with which to carry out an odious operation on several feet of black sausage.

"Ah, Barney. I wonder if you could stop what you're doing and pop along to the chemist?"

"Chemist, guv? Don't tell me Alice has run out of disinfectant again?"

"It's—er—Chubb's prescription."

"Oh, yeah, I saw the vet come and go. What's the verdict?"

"Just a touch of *Virus Caninculus*. I gather there's a lot of it about."

"Cor, that sounds bad."

"It'll be quite a large bottle of medicine, Barney. Probably of a disagreeable colour. I shouldn't take the stopper off and sniff it if I were you. And Barney ..."

"Yes, guv?"

Mr Peacock winked broadly and then, because he wasn't sure Barney had noticed, he winked again. "On your way back, Barney, you will have a slight mishap. Catch your foot on a stone, perhaps."

"Come again? Why should I do a silly thing like that?"

"Most unfortunate! You'll have forgotten to place the bottle securely in your pocket. Rather careless, Barney. There is the bottle in your hand and out it slips."

"Slips, guv?"

"Slips, Barney. Before you can save it, it drops on a deserted stretch of pavement and smashes to pieces. Of course, being a responsible member of the community you clear up the mess as best you can. And Barney, don't bring any stray dogs home with you—the medicine is probably laced with aniseed or something equally foul. Cut along, there's a good fellow. Nobody, in your absence, will interfere with that gruesome travesty of a breakfast you're experimenting on!"

5

"What are they doing out there?" asked Barney Stoat, later that morning. "Filming the Battle of Dunkirk?"

"It is rather inconvenient, Barney," conceded Mr Peacock. "But essential as a device for, shall we say, pulling the wool over the eyes of over-inquisitive onlookers. As you know, we still have our regular clientele in and out."

"Not many of them come in for breakfast," grumbled Barney.

"No wonder!" snapped Alice.

Barney grinned. "Wait till you get me lunch. Hasenbraten mit Rahmsauce—saddle of hare in cream sauce to you, guv. Matter of fact, I shot the hare meself this morning, after I'd got rid of the you-know-what."

They'd decided to keep their duplicity over Mr Whelp's prescription to themselves. As Barney had put it, Alice would no doubt have opened Chubb's mouth with a set of fire tongs and emptied the vile bottle into his throat without compunction.

"By the way," said Mr Peacock, changing the subject. "Has anyone seen Chubb lately?"

"I took him breakfast," said Barney. "You sure that vet was right in his diagnosis, guv? Couldn't be foot and mouth disease, like? Seems off his food."

"*What* food?" sneered Alice. "If you're referring to that ghastly black sausage, it seems to have affected his brain. He actually *growled* at me through his kennel door."

"Look here, you two," said Mr Peacock, irritably. "All this chit-chat about cookery and so on . . . you do realise that the Princess and her entourage are due tonight? And we are all, so to speak, at the centre of an International Intrigue. For the moment, let us go about our ordinary business with discretion, and—if I am not demanding *too* much—a reasonable degree of peace and quietude?"

Through the windows came an uproar resembling the storming of the Bastille.

Barney said, "You'd better tell them lot that, guv! The way they're carrying on, the locals will think flying saucers have landed."

"I found a TV cameraman treading on our tubers," said Alice. "And the police have got their silly fence tangled up with my washing line."

"How many for lunch, guv?"

"I believe, Barney, the police and the television crew have brought sandwiches."

"What, cheese and pickle? The trouble with the English public, guv, is they got no palate."

"Barney," frowned Mr Peacock irascibly. "I do wish you would, for the time being, set aside your newly acquired, if admirable, culinary skill and pay attention. The Superintendent is rather worried. Apparently, heavy snow is forecast for this evening. Due, in fact, at about the same time as the entourage is scheduled to arrive. Could complicate matters—it is imperative, I understand, that the Princess be driven without fuss or clamour to Dover in the morning to catch the Royal Yacht, cunningly disguised, I gather, as a coaster carrying coal. We must be prepared for any emergency. It is even possible that the Royal Party will favour us with a slightly longer stay than was at first envisaged."

At this, Barney's eyes glazed over and one could practically see Glockensteinian recipes printed in miniature on his pupils. "Well, if it comes to the worst, the cops could get 'em out by chopper, couldn't they?"

"Hardly in a snowstorm, Barney. But, as a matter of fact, the Super did mention his contingency plan. There *is* a helicopter standing by. Top Secret, of course, but I know I can rely on your discretion. And it was most astute of you to mention a film about Dunkirk. You were, shall we say, warm, Barney. The Home Office, however, opted for 'Colditz'—with, as you can see, the full co-operation of the BBC."

BBC

"Blimey," said Barney. "And they're using the Highway Inn as a back drop? What about turrets and things?"

"Papier mâché, I believe. Amazing what they can do with papier mâché."

Alice said, "Ridiculous! Why couldn't they have sent the young Princess home by submarine, or something? And if we're going to have this place full of silly policemen dressed up as Nazis, goose-stepping all over my floor, I shall pack my bags. Ridiculous!"

The day was long and grey and heavy with the threat of snow.

For Chubb, however, it was remarkably short. He had woken briefly that morning, mostly to disdain his continental breakfast. Then he had bestirred himself again at lunchtime and decided that, after all, he might as well nibble one end of Barney's odious black sausage. After that, upon his warm mattress and with Alice's electric blanket in pleasant and soporific working order, the only possible thing to disturb him next would be the tantalising drift towards his grievously blocked nose of supper aromas (unless, in the suddenly topsy-turvy world, it was lunch).

So it was that the Basset Hound at last sneezed once, opened his eyes and then, with a quite heroic thrust of aching limbs, succeeded in pushing his heavy body up on his forepaws—and naturally his nose followed.

For some reason there was no sniff of food. At first, Chubb put this down to the effects of his infirmity and, not unduly discouraged, gave his door a weakened but determined shove.

The door moved slowly and stiffly before the catch secured it open. He was at once aware of distant sounds—the shout of human voices, the march of feet—the tumult, in fact, of invasion and plunder, some alien and large booted foe, apparently, marching upon the Highway Inn.

More alarming still, as Chubb could see, the doorway was almost entirely blocked by snow. Only a moonlit chink appeared at the top, giving access to a piercing draught which at once produced a fit of coughing. Fortunately, however, a pair of familiar eyes arrived in the slit and there was the scent of food, of sorts.

Not, to be sure, the kind of food which Chubb normally favoured, but in his present state, malnutrition could prove even more deadly than *Virus Caninculus*. Once one had acquired the taste, one simply gulped down the extraordinary substance, not dwelling too long on its doubtful ingredients.

"You look nice and snug down there, Chubb, old mate," said Barney. "Brought you some more black sausage—Glockenstein's favourite dish, you know. What caviar is to the Russians, and stuffed frog is to the Frenchies, so black sausage is a rare delicacy to the Glockensteinians. Got yourself a bit snowed up, eh? I'll slip the plate through the crack. Got it? Oh, and seeing it was your supper, I messed about a bit with the recipe. Slipped in a shot of brandy! How's that? You'll hardly notice the taste of the onions!"

The plate slid through on the ridge of icy snow and landed conveniently at Chubb's feet. He nibbled cautiously, feeling that *no* nourishment, however ill judged and badly cooked, should be allowed to languish uneaten in the corner of a kennel.

In due course a second pair of eyes presented themselves in the snowy slit of door. "I say, old fellow," said Mr Peacock. "You're snowed up! We'll have to dig you out before you vanish altogether. I'll see if I can borrow a spade from one of the Superintendent's men. The entourage has just arrived. The Superintendent had to rush up a tractor from somewhere—disguised as a tank. Papier mâché, you know. They've succeeded in towing the Princess's Mercedes into the car park and hustling her indoors. Look here, old chap, once I've dug you out I see no reason why we can't creep off together to the snuggery. The Superintendent is busily occupied discussing some script or other with a BBC producer."

To Mr Peacock's astonishment, Chubb answered, "A dog has his duty, Inspector. On the whole, not without gratitude for your suggestion, I would prefer to remain at my post. Vigilance, you know."

"Oh very well," said Mr Peacock, disappointedly. "Though how much vigilance you can maintain through a gap less than an inch wide I cannot imagine! Not only that, but Barney, Alice and I have done a little vigilating of our own all day. Calling upon you, Chubb, to attend to your needs and enquire after your health. Each time, several raps on your kennel roof have brought no response but snores!"

"Not *snores* Inspector. Rasps, more likely. I can assure you that my ears were not asleep and, as for my nose, congested though it may be, it has remained attuned to every event."

"Very well," sighed Mr Peacock. "Then I shall retire alone and listen to my new set of Bavarian dances on the hi-fi. A pity—you might have met the Princess Katerina in person. She is as delightful as we could have hoped, despite her touch of mischief. Even Alice has noticed how pretty she looks in her fur hood and cape. As for the rest, personally I'm not enamoured, Chubb. Herr Fink, the gentleman in charge, has a twitch in his cheek. He has already complained at the lack of *schnapps*—a drink, I believe, much favoured in Glockenstein. My oversight, alas—I should have laid in a crate or two. There is a fellow called Franz, who drove the car—until the Super's papier mâché tank took over. Candidly, old chap, he is of such sinister demeanour that had he arrived as a tourist, trying to book into the hotel, I would have redirected him to a less exacting pub out on the Dover Road!

"The Princess also has a bodyguard. I rather fancy he was once a strong man in a circus. Not uncivil, Chubb. I would not say he was *uncivil*, but he does have an annoying habit of pushing open doors with one massive shoulder and eyeing anybody he happens to meet as if about to snatch a Luger from his pocket. Difficult to understand why the Princess needs a human bodyguard, when, after all, she has the Dobermann. I should watch out for him, if I were you Chubb. A proud and stubborn beast, slinking about like the Hound of the Baskervilles, sniffing into every corner and loping off in disappointment because he's failed to locate an assassin under the floorboards! Name of Heinz, after the beans.

"Lastly, there is Gertrude, the Princess's female chaperone. No doubt an agreeable enough lady, but her voice is shrill and quite unintelligible. No love lost between her and Alice—I happened to overhear a totally garbled dispute about the colour of the Princess's sheets. She has a strong preference for pink, and poor Alice made up her bed in blue. Trust Alice to get *something* wrong! That's all I can tell you for the time being, old fellow. Good night."

With that, Mr Peacock slammed shut the kennel door and left Chubb to his dark thoughts—and a further, purely experimental, nibble of Barney Stoat's slightly modified Glockensteinian recipe.

Chubb was still cautiously licking his chops when there came a rustle and snuffle immediately outside his door.

With another mighty effort of his declining

powers, Chubb succeeded in opening it. The bank of snow immediately outside had vanished and, in the reflected moonlight, he saw the head of a dog.

Not the Princess's Dobermann, Chubb observed with some relief. (When he should encounter the creature called Heinz, he would prefer it to be on his own ground—with some possibility of strategic withdrawal!)

It was Rex the police dog, with whom Chubb had had, from time to time, certain investigations in common. A not unfriendly, nor entirely unworthy member of the canine classes, Chubb remembered. Young and brash he might be, but he usually showed a proper deference.

"Why, Mr Chubb, sir! I thought I might find you here. What on earth are you doing in a kennel?"

Chubb stifled a sneeze. "Special duties," he said. "Advance Observation Post."

"And very nice too, if I may say so, Mr Chubb, sir. No better than you deserve of course. Soft mattress? Heated blanket? Just as it should be, Mr Chubb. Great believer in respect for rank, myself. As for the likes of me, a bare, cold kennel is sufficient. A plain straw mat, Mr Chubb. Tin of meat once a day and water slopped into the same bowl! I wonder—not meaning to intrude Mr Chubb, sir—could I pop in for a little chat? Allowing for the differences of rank, we may be once again assigned to the same case. The Princess Katerina? A possible International Incident? Special Branch stuff, of course.

No wonder they've roped you in, Mr Chubb."

"Umph!" said Chubb. "Try not to get snow on my bed, young fellow, and close the door behind you. You do it with your nose."

"I've got it, sir," said the police dog, turning about, slithering backwards through the door, then deftly snapping it shut behind him.

6

Having joined Chubb on the mattress, Rex snuffled apprehensively in the utter darkness. "A good thing, Mr Chubb, that dogs such as us have our noses. How else would we see anything? I sometimes wonder how our superiors and betters expect us to carry out onerous duties—you must agree, Mr Chubb, sir, that the duties are onerous—in black holes, and worse. Talking of noses, have you by any chance caught a cold?"

"Grumph," said Chubb. "I would have thought my condition obvacious—quite obvacious. It was necessary to receive urgent medical attention. The well known vet, you know, Mr Whelp, breaking his journey to the world famous Dog Clinic in Berne—Switzerland, I understand—and diagnosing *Virus Caninculus*."

"A lot of it about, sir. I myself had a touch of it. The cure is, of course, worse than the disease. Strange how devoted the humans appear to be to pills and odious liquids in bottles. When it comes to food, Mr Chubb, *one* tin of indifferent nourishment per day is expected to keep our coats in good trim. But medicine, is—ah, medicine! *Four* doses, and they'd make it five if we didn't bare our teeth in protest." Rex sniffed. "While still on the subject of smells and tastes, Mr Chubb, if I'm not speaking out of turn, there is a mysterious and not entirely disagreeable odour hanging about your person."

"Black sausage," said Chubb. "With onions."

"I must say, Mr Chubb, sir, I'm rather partial to onions."

"Then help yourself," said Chubb. It crossed the Basset Hound's mind that a dog with a partiality for onions must leave much to be desired, not only in his nature but in his efficiency, but he let it pass. Neither, during all the munchings and scrunchings, did the police dog once pause to delight his nose with the whiff of brandy lingering about Barney Stoat's continental left overs. Alsatians, alas, rarely appreciated such subtleties.

"Very tasty, Mr Chubb, sir," said Rex, at last. "Now, down to business, if I may make so bold. I am here, so to speak, *ex officio*. That is, sir, I have no wish to intrude upon your manor. On the other hand, it occurs to me that, since you are not quite in the pink of condition, you will scarcely have had the chance to come to grips, so to speak, with the events taking place above. For instance, sir, the Princess Katerina and her entourage..."

In the darkness Chubb permitted himself a brief, throaty chuckle. "With greater experience, you will learn that catching villains is not always a matter of grabbing trouser legs and the like! A really successful detective dog—and here I may modestly describe myself as such—denies himself such crudities. Deduction, observation, the drawing together of intangillous clues—these are what count. For instance, I was placed here, in what has been designated my Advanced Observation Post, not to while away the hours, but to appraise myself—in my own fashion—of all momentous happenings. As to the entourage, save your breath, young fellow. The Glockensteinian gentleman called Herr Fink—he with the twitch. The shifty chauffeur, Franz. The bodyguard, Gustave, who opens doors with his shoulder. Ah, there is the little Princess herself, of course, who prefers pink sheets to blue, and her somewhat querulous chaperone, Gertrude. Last but not least, young friend, we have in our midst the formidable Dobermann called Heinz—after the beans, of course, who, I am quite sure, possesses considerable conceit and is under the mistaken impression that he can slink about at will and rule the roost. I presume, young fellow, that if we are to discover a terrorist with designs against the fair Princess Katerina, it is your opinion that we need maintain our vigilance no further than the members of this entourage. There is, to put it another way, a cuckoo in the breast?"

There was a gasp of admiration from the young

police dog. "Good gracious, Mr Chubb, sir! How do you do it—and down here in the dark, under several feet of snow?"

Chubb coughed. "Smells, young fellow. It's all in the smells. Remember, during what will no doubt be quite a tolerable career as a police dog, that *smells* are what matter. I well remember the Case of the Chinese Junk . . . if there were time, I would relate it to you as an object lesson."

"I think we have the time, Mr Chubb. And this, if I may say so, is an extraordinarily warm mattress. On the whole, it might be indiscreet of me—so long as I am not outstaying my welcome—to return too hastily to the wintry world above. There is also a further embarrassment—my handler, you know. Unfortunately, in the interests of greater mobility, I

endeavoured successfully to disengage myself from the tug of his lead. You know the trick, sir—merely a matter of catching them off guard. I thought I could be of greater value to the Kent Constabulary, not to mention the State of Glockenstein, were I not for ever choking on a chain. Not, mind you, that when we have apprehended the would-be assassin we shall get a word of thanks. For me, Mr Chubb, sir—at least a week's solitary confinement on dog biscuits and water. By the way, should it be of passing interest, I managed to worry off my collar—you know how it is done, sir—and jettison both it and lead near one of the dustbins behind the Inn, hopefully concealed with snow. But, Mr Chubb, you mentioned, I believe, a Chinese Junk?"

Chubb's bones creaked a little as he indulged in one of his characteristic shrugs. "If you insist, young fellow. I was on a special assignment at the time—Hong Kong, you know. The Hong Kong police, at that point, were in need of a little advice from Scotland Yard. They had an unfortunate tendency to employ coolies as detectives—hats gave them away at once, not to mention the manner in which they trotted about as if pulling carts. However that may be, the Superintendent of the Hong Kong police came to me one day and said, 'Chubb, my friend, we have arrested two suspects, one of whom is indubitably a drug trafficker. At our briefing conference this morning we could not agree upon which was the villain. Have you possibly the time to interview them for us?'

"Now, at the time I was feeling sanguine. Sanguine, is how I felt. I had just breakfasted off an excellent meal supplied by the Superintendent and his staff. Chicken noodle soup, I remember, followed by a meat dish of exquisite perfectiousness. So I agreed to do as the Superintendent requested. One, I recall, was a shifty personage. Chinaman, of course. Grimacing teeth, crooked eyes, hands furtively feeling for a knife concealed in his clothing.

"The other fellow was quite different—suave is the word. Suave, young fellow. He greeted me with a most civil pat on the head and claimed to have a partiality for the properly bred Basset Hound. Face as honest as the moon, a whiff about him of a Chinese rose garden."

Rex the police dog interrupted, with due deference. "I see, Mr Chubb, sir. It was all in the smells. Of course, you advised the arrest of the first villain? No doubt with your highly tuned nose you picked up the scent of ships' rope, the acrid tang of a smuggler's junk, the obnoxious odour of heroin?"

"Ah," said Chubb out of the blackness, his wheezy chuckle shaking the kennel walls. "You have fallen into my trap, young fellow. In a case of this kind, a case requiring—if I may so put it—a more than usual perspicaciousness, one does not jump to conclusions. *Obviousness* is not enough. Certainly not obviousness."

"My word, Mr Chubb, sir," gasped the police

dog, "Are you saying that it was the *other* one whose arrest you secured? The Chinese gentleman who smelt of roses and, even more important, patted your head? Baffling, Mr Chubb, sir!"

"Quite," said Chubb. "But then, it is not always *smells* that matter. Occasionally it is *no* smells."

"Quite beyond me, sir," sighed the police dog, wondering if the Basset Hound had noticed that he was quietly rummaging about in a corner in search of a last fragment of black sausage. "Most, if I may say so, incredulous."

"Grumph!" said Chubb. "With due attention to the advice of others, you will grasp the dictum, young fellow. Remember, not always *smells*, but *no smells*. It cannot be said too often. To take, for example, the case I have just described... no one who reeked of heroin, and Chinese junks, and, incidentally, dustbins and the indigestible contents of rice bowls could possibly be a villain. I also happened to hear that the second suspect—I believe his name was Wing Wong—had a detestation for dogs. Patting my head, in fact, amply demonstrated the despicable creature's utterest complicity."

"Well, Mr Chubb, sir," said Rex, creeping back disappointed at having discovered no further trace of Glockensteinian sausage, with or without onion. "So it is your opinion that in our present investigations we should not rely entirely on *smells*."

"Not *entirely*," agreed Chubb, out of the dark.

"For instance, as of course you know, sir, the

bodyguard, Gustave, has no lobes to his ears and there is I would say, a distinct odour of gunpowder about his person."

"Fireworks, perhaps. The Glockensteinians are rather partial to fireworks."

"And Franz the chauffeur, Mr Chubb, spends much of his time, I noticed, prowling round the Princess's Mercedes in the car park. Possibly, I thought, sir, rigging up some explosive device."

"Unlikely," grunted Chubb.

The police dog was evidently lost in thought. "That leaves us with Herr Fink, sir. He does, in my opinion, have a tendency to loiter near the dustbins. Or Gertrude, the Princess's chaperone. Smells of moth balls! I suppose, since in a fashion he is one of us, we can eliminate the Dobermann, Heinz? Mind you, Mr Chubb, he is probably quite capable of an atrocity. My eyes may have deceived me, but I was quite convinced that for supper tonight they gave him a whole sheep, frozen, no doubt. An ugly customer, Mr Chubb. A very ugly customer indeed. Have to be watched, if I may say so."

"Or *smelt,* young fellow," said Chubb, unexpectedly. "I have an impression that our friend Heinz is, at this moment, not far—sniffing at the door in fact! I presume that by now the hound has learned of my reputation."

At this, the kennel shook as if there was a live rhinoceros immediately below trying to get out, but alas it was Rex trembling in every bone.

However, to his great credit, he got a hold on himself and said: "Leave him to me, Mr Chubb, sir. This is a job for the local force. Who's afraid of a mere Dobermann? Why, sir, I don't wish to boast, I could take on three of the likes of him—before breakfast. Just you stay in here. Lie doggo, sir. Leave him to me!"

With this, Rex pushed open the exit with his nose, slithered out in a shower of snow, and let the door close behind him.

7

Despite his brave words, Rex the police dog, out in the moonlit snow, found his own stout heart beating so loudly that a set of drums would scarcely have made themselves heard against the competition.

He could see the fearsome Dobermann, Heinz, prowling in circles, sinuous body as lithe as a leopard's. The huge collar he wore jangled with decorations obviously awarded him for deeds of past valour, such as eating enemies of Glockenstein whole, no doubt. He had scarcely a stump of cropped tail, but he used this to good effect, hindquarters twitching almost more arrogantly than his long haughty nose, as if to suggest that if only his breeders had allowed a fuller flourish, he could have knocked a donkey off its feet.

The beast came to a halt at last, gazing so imperiously at Rex that the Alsatian felt himself obliged to say, in order to keep his teeth from chattering, "Ah, Herr Heinz. How do you do?"

In response the Dobermann raised one front paw in salute, "Heil!" he growled. Then, "Ach so, you wish to say that you have discovered the Princess Katerina?"

"Are you saying, Mein Herr, that Her Highness has eluded your surveillance?"

The Dobermann sneered down from his great height. "Hah! Do you suppose, young dog, that I am here to bark at the moon, perhaps? Or would I leave my place by the fire in the Inn merely to pass the time, how you say, conversing with any young pup who happened to pass by?"

Rex discovered that indignation is sometimes an excellent cure for trepidation. He drew himself up to his full height, only a foot or so beneath the tinkling collar. "Begging your pardon, sir, it may have escaped your notice that I am a police dog on duty.

I am sure you appreciate that it is always our wish to be of assistance to foreign tourists."

The awe-inspiring nose hovered nearer. "Hah! Your English police employ the dog with feeble eyesight? How does he see the fox? I am not the tourist but the guardian of a princess."

Rex succeeded in reaching within four inches of the Dobermann's nose. "Then there would seem to have been a slip up somewhere, sir. You inadvertently fell asleep in the saloon bar, perhaps? Not your fault, sir. Our English hospitality overwhelmed you, no doubt."

The Dobermann's stump of tail twitched again. "We waste time in, how you put it, the chit-chat. If, as you claim, you are the police dog, let us go together at once in search. You are at the disposal, yah?"

"It will be an honour, sir," said Rex, their noses now no more than *two* inches apart.

"An honour indeed, young dog." Heinz gave his enormous collar an extra shake. "As you see, I wear the Silver Cross, with Oak Leaf. Also the Gold Medallion for valour. Not to mention the Bronze Bone of Glockenstein itself—a rare distinction, I tell you, awarded to only two of my ancestors. But as for the Princess Katerina, sometimes I would rather guard the flying bird! Mein Gott! First she visit the coal mine and we find her with black face in the shaft. In London, during the banquet at your Guild Hall, I myself save her as she try to climb the Nelson

Column! Perhaps, next we should put our noses in the drain, yah?"

Their noses now practically touching, Rex felt a wave of sympathy for the Dobermann which was spoilt only when the haughty Heinz went on, "We must search the nooks and the crannies. Tell me, young dog, what was that hole out of which you crept?"

"Rabbits," explained Rex, remarkably quick-witted. "In passing, having a spare moment, sir, just rabbits."

"Ah, the rabbit. So you like to hunt, young dog? Myself also, when my exhausting duties permit. But for me the Wild Pig. However, even the Princess Katerina, I think, will not have hidden away in the rabbit hole! It has occurred to me that there may be the enemy in our midst. A villain in disguise, perhaps, who is doing the kidnap. We sniff him out, young dog, then we tear him to the pieces, yah?"

Rex avoided looking too closely at the bared teeth gleaming, in the moonlight. "Always glad to be of service, sir. As to a dastardly villain in disguise, I think we may eliminate the persons from the BBC. They are busy with their film. 'Colditz Castle', you know. I take it, sir, that you know the place well? As for the policemen on duty—unthinkable, of course. But I have been wondering, Herr Heinz, about the figure amongst the trees bordering the car park. He can scarcely have escaped your notice, sir? Moving furtively in the direction of the Inn, wearing the uniform of a World War Two German soldier. Not I presume, one of your entourage?"

"Certainly not!" said the Dobermann, just that moment spotting the suspicious shadow across the snow. "The entourage does not wear the uniform."

"He ought to be apprehended, if I may be so bold as to suggest it, sir. If you will kindly take a leg, I will try for an arm."

"Excellent!" growled Heinz. "When we make an arrest, young dog, I shall see that you are suitably rewarded. The Bronze Leaf of Glockenstein, perhaps. With Stem. Let us seize the fellow at once—yah?"

Meanwhile, rumours of the Princess's disappearance had run rife and Mr Peacock, attempting to spend a quiet evening with his Bavarian dances, was soon interrupted by a string of visitors.

First of all, Barney Stoat sidled in, face ominous. "Come in, Barney," said the retired Inspector, quite unnecessarily. "Close the door behind you, there's a good chap. More than enough racket coming through the window. I must say, I do think the BBC are taking things rather far, don't you? The device of covering operations with a subterfuge—the film sequence—is splendid in principle. But, really, this incessant mortar fire, even with dummy cartridges, is a little wearing on the nerves. And so far as I can see, the Dobermann, even though I wouldn't call him my favourite breed of dog, with the help of our weight-lifter friend, Gustave, is perfectly capable of taking good care of the Princess Katerina without *quite* such an elaborate charade."

For some reason Barney did not appear reassured. "Yeah, well, you see guv, it's the schnapps."

"The *what*, Barney?"

"Schnapps. Didn't I get round to telling you? I managed to lift a couple of bottles from the supermarket in town. In a manner of speaking, like. Not my fault, though, that Herr Fink and Co get squiffy and spill their glasses smack into the plate we put out for the Hound of the Baskervilles."

"I don't quite see your drift, Barney," frowned Mr Peacock.

"Well, he fell fast asleep, didn't he? And that so

called bodyguard, Gustave, is sprawled over his table, singing the Glockensteinian National Anthem. And, meanwhile, what's happened to the Princess Katerina? Gorn."

"Good gracious! Where?"

"Meaning no disrespect guv, that's a daft question isn't it? Nobody knows. Whole place is in an uproar. I overheard the BBC bloke say that the best thing was to fit it all into the script so the cops're swarming like ants up them papier mâché turrets. Somebody's going to break his neck!"

"Good heavens! I must get to the scene at once..."

"Oh, I shouldn't bother, guv. More than enough clowns chasing each other as it is!" Barney slid a shade closer, his face taking on the furtive expression he'd once used when picking people's pockets, before Mr Peacock had turned him into an honest man. "Better, if you ask me, guv, if everybody cooled down and used a bit of loaf. *I* can tell you something that might help."

"What's that Barney?"

"The chauffeur done it! The one called Franz."

"Done *what*? You mean—abducted the Princess? What makes you think that?"

"Mind if I take a pew, guv? Ta. It's like this, see? He's not one of them, not one of the entourage, I mean. The way I figure it, he's the real Franz's double. An impostor, like. Probably murdered the real chauffeur and hid him in the boot of the

Mercedes. That would account for why he spends most of his time prowling round the car park keeping an eye on the body, so to speak."

"Most interesting Barney. What led you to this somewhat sinister conclusion?"

"Easy," said Barney, sprawling at his ease among Chubb's velvet cushions. "It was at nosh-up time tonight. I'd got this nice little meal going—Krautfleisch—pork with sauerkraut to you, guv, with a dash of garlic, and what do you think?"

"Oh, do get on with it, Barney."

"Well this bloke, Franz, or whatever his real name is, comes into the kitchen and nudges me elbow. Know what he says, in perfect English? 'Herr Stoat' (that was the only bit of German he used) 'do you think I could have egg and chips for me dinner?' I ask you, guv. Egg and chips! And him supposed to be a Glockensteinian. And there's worse to come. Wanting to be obliging, like, I knock him up the eggs and chips, then he brings his plate back—and know what he wants for afters? Instead of the Kirschenmehlspeise—Cherry Dessert to you, guv—he practically begs for rhubarb tart and custard!"

Mr Peacock nodded sagely, "This does sound rather significant, Barney. Have you conveyed your suspicions to the Superintendent of Police?"

"Who, him? He's missing, and all. I ask you, the Law in this country is coming to a pretty pass when the bloke supposed to be in charge scarpers off to Bingo or whatever."

"I shouldn't think..." began Mr Peacock, when there was a second peremptory rap on the snuggery door.

Four persons entered at Mr Peacock's invitation. There was Herr Fink himself, white faced and twitching even more than usual. Beside him was Gertrude, the Princess's chaperone, sobbing into a pink handkerchief. The chauffeur, the possibly bogus Franz, hovered in their wake. The fourth person, Gustave the bodyguard, now more or less sober, came in last, shut the door with his shoulder and leaned on it like an extra wall.

"Something must be done," said Herr Fink. "Where is the Princess? Not anywhere in the hotel. Not up in the balloon. Not in the thin air—nein?"

"My dear Herr Fink..." said Mr Peacock, and was yet again interrupted.

On this occasion it was the police sergeant who, as Mr Peacock remembered, was Rex's handler, tie crooked, mouth more crooked still. "Mr Peacock, sir, would you happen to have seen my dog? Slipped his chain, been missing for hours. With respect, sir, I've been thinking. Your Basset Hound..."

Mr Peacock bristled. "Look here, Sergeant, just because you can't seem to keep that Alsatian under proper control, there's no need to cast aspersions. As a matter of fact, Chubb is in sick quarters. He hasn't stirred all day, except to take a little occasional light nourishment."

"Meaning no offence, sir," said the Sergeant

glumly. "I was only asking, like. And I'm going to have to explain to the Super."

"Hardly a matter of immediate concern, Sergeant. From all accounts it seems that he, too, is mysteriously missing . . ."

It was then that Mr Peacock saw his golden chance. *He* would take charge—at least until the Superintendent got back from Bingo, or wherever. Run the whole show, squash the forces of terrorism, earn the undying gratitude of the King of Glockenstein himself!

"Hah!" he said, deciding that the thing to do was to speak with the Voice of Authority, show these fellows what the English police were made of. "Mein Herren, Mein Fraulein, and—er—Barney. This is how we shall conduct the investigation from now on."

All eyes were upon Mr Peacock with new respect: Herr Fink's face twitched attentively, Gertrude ceased to weep, Franz (impostor or not) clicked his heels and bowed his head as if about to be shot by a firing squad.

"Now, as to our immediate plan of action," said Mr Peacock. "I propose that in the course of our briefing, we should take into account . . . oh, drat it! Who is it *now*?"

The door flew open with such violence that even the formidable Gustave was practically thrown off his feet.

It was hard, at first, to decide whether the new

invader was a snowman who had miraculously come to life, or something equally wonderful recently emerged from a time machine.

Only when the snow on its person began to thaw could it be confirmed that the figure wore the uniform of a Nazi soldier, battledress torn and tattered, helmet askew, swastika on one arm hanging by a thread.

"Good heavens!" exclaimed Mr Peacock. "Superintendent, have you had some sort of accident?"

"Accident fiddlesticks!" The now slightly more recognisable apparition steamed indignantly. "Someone shall answer for this. Tell me, Sergeant, have you by any chance mislaid your dog?"

The Sergeant paled visibly as he stood to attention. "Merely on—um—routine patrol, sir."

"Ha! I shall see that it is destroyed! Now, Herr Fink—perhaps you will be good enough to inform me when you last set eyes on that beast of yours, the Dobermann?"

Herr Fink turned scarlet and clenched his fists. "The beast! You refer to our worthy Heinz as the *beast*? Mein Gott! I will inform your Home Secretary of this insult. I will seek the audience with your Queen!"

The Superintendent eventually succeeded in unstrapping his German helmet, which he plonked down on Mr Peacock's desk with a thud. "And that Basset Hound of yours, Inspector. I suppose, by some dereliction of duty, you failed to chain it up as I requested. At least *four* dogs committed the outrage, making a patently unprovoked attack upon me in the course of my duty . . ."

Mr Peacock, face of an even deeper hue than Herr Fink's, was about to splutter a protest when, unexpectedly, Barney Stoat flared up as if somebody had just put a match to him. "Come off it, Super. You must have been seeing double, like everybody else around this dump tonight. Chubb's in his kennel, where you more or less shoved him, probably dying of misery. And what you haven't got round to telling us yet is what you're doing, done up like a dog's dinner in that gear, sort of stormtrooper cum scarecrow."

"I'll have none of your cheek, young man!" glared the Superintendent. "It just so happens the producer johnny from the BBC asked if I would stand in as an extra. For the film, of course. Naturally, I obliged at once. It appears that some of the original cast got snowed up on their way to the location. Moreover, it occurred to me that a disguise would assist me in maintaining an extra sharp vigilance from the towers of Colditz Castle."

"Blimey!" chuckled Barney Stoat. "You mean, you was playing a bit-part as a goon? No wonder the country's in the state it is. Shouldn't be surprised if they call on the Commissioner next and ask him to dress up as Hitler himself!"

"Silence!" bellowed the Superintendent beginning to peel off the ripped German tunic, until he remembered that he was wearing only his undies beneath. "To work at once. I take it that, in my temporary absence from the Command Post, nobody has yet succeeded in locating the Princess? On the whole, Inspector, I think we can manage quite adequately without your well-intentioned, but perhaps not wholly effective, involvement. I suggest you stay here out of the cold—as Strategic Reserve, so to speak—and continue writing your memoirs."

8

Morning arrived at last. At first light, the snow had scattered away out of the sky, leaving patches of blue. The gutters of the Inn under the papier mâché turrets dripped incessantly. The vehicles in the car park lost their snow hats.

Heinz the Dobermann was awake and on the prowl, and not in the best of tempers. After a short interview with Herr Fink, Gustave the Princess's bodyguard had emerged from the littered bar, red of face, with bloodshot eyes, and snatched Heinz's breakfast plate from beneath his nose. In addition, Franz the chauffeur had given him a sly, if slightly risky, kick on his way out.

So, on the whole, Heinz was not entirely sorry to find himself temporarily out of immediate reach as he slunk round the edge of the car park. So far he had picked up no scent of the Princess Katerina—and neither was he in the best of condition after the previous night's sojourn in the saloon bar.

If the wintry morning outside was bleak in the extreme, it was nothing compared with the atmosphere in Mr Peacock's snuggery. The retired Inspector had succeeded at last in freeing himself from Herr Fink's terrible twitch and latest spluttering accusations. He had also, for the moment, managed to extricate Barney and Alice from the interrogations they had suffered for the past hour.

Barney in particular was explosively indignant. "Blimey, guv. You'd think they was the Gestapo! All they needed was knuckle dusters. I know it's hard lines, losing their Princess, but what am I supposed to have done—bricked her up behind the fireplace?"

Alice was still dabbing her eyes with a damp hanky. "Most insulting! That woman, Gertrude, searched my bedroom from top to bottom. I kept *telling* her that Princess Katerina was *not* in the closet where I hang my clothes for special occasions. And that I'd temporarily mislaid the key."

Barney Stoat said, "You'd better find it, Alice. If you got a nice black dress going spare you're going to need it, Any minute now we'll probably be taken out, put against a wall, and shot."

"Yes, well," said Mr Peacock. "I hope it will come as some comfort that I appear after all, to be in charge." He rubbed his hands with evident satisfaction. "The Superintendent is temporarily indisposed—delayed shock, I presume. The mauling he got, of course, whilst he was dressed up as—ah—a goon. Now, whatever grievous fate awaits us, we must carry on, as Herr Fink would put it, with the stiff upper lip. Bound to be some delay, before the Princess is safely recovered. Meanwhile the hotel is bulging at the seams with extra visitors stranded by the snow. I rather hope, by the way, that we are to be recompensed. A suitable fee from the BBC, for instance, and perhaps a contribution from the Kent Constabulary's Benevolent Fund. At the moment Herr Fink is dragging everybody out of bed to be interrogated. Barney, can you possibly manage forty-two breakfasts?"

"Yeah," nodded Barney. "Raw eggs, tomato juice, with a dash of Vodka. It was quite a party last night. There are big enough hangovers in this place to make the Dover cliffs look like mere wrinkles on the landscape."

Mr Peacock drummed at his desk with a pencil. "Now that we are together for the moment, away from the immediate surveillance of the Glockenstein Authorities, I think we should get our priorities right. Do you realise that we've scarcely given a thought to Chubb? In some ways, the poor old fellow will be sorry he missed all this. One does, on such occasions, miss his sage and not entirely unwise observations. In a manner of speaking, of course," he added hastily.

Alice sniffed. "There are times when that Basset Hound and I have had our ups and downs, but I don't mind admitting that, compared with their dreadful Dobermann, Chubb is as gentle and harmless as a kitten in a basket."

"I'm glad you've got round to seeing him in that light, Alice," said Mr Peacock. "I take it, Barney, that despite your recent ordeal it has not entirely escaped your attention that Chubb, too, will be wanting breakfast?"

"Got it all organised, guv. As a matter of fact, I was on me way to his kennel with a plate of good old English sausages when that gorilla, Gustave, put out his jack boot and tripped me up."

"Capital, Barney!" said Mr Peacock. "I presume the sausages were saved? Cut along, then. I'm afraid you may need a shovel to gain access to his door."

Barney was gone less than ten minutes, returning with the untouched and lukewarm sausages and a face the colour of chalk. "I don't know how I'm going to say this, guv."

"What is it Barney? And *do* put that plate down. You're not trying to tell us that something has happened to Chubb?"

"I dunno, to tell the truth. The poor old mutt is buried so deep. I managed to clear a way to his kennel, though. Didn't want to give the old dog a sudden icy draught so I kicked his door and hollered: 'Wakey, wakey, old mate. Breakfast up!' And you know what? No answer, not a peep."

"Well, perhaps he was oversleeping," said Mr Peacock. "After all nearly everybody else is. So next, I take it, you did get round to opening his door?"

"Sorry, guv. Couldn't bring meself to do it. In

that eerie silence I felt like I was hammering on a grave."

"Ridiculous, Barney!" said Mr Peacock. "Oh, give me that plate—I'll take it along. Chubb will listen to me."

When Mr Peacock's returning shadow fell across the foggy window, they could see at once that his normally brisk figure was bent in dejection and the sausages were stone cold.

"What happened, guv?" asked Barney. "No, on second thoughts, don't tell us! You knocked, same as me. And when you didn't get no answer, you kicked his door open—right? Don't tell us what you... saw!"

Mr Peacock shook his head vaguely, "As a matter of fact Barney ... that is to say, I tried—really I did, Barney—but, like yourself, somehow I couldn't bring myself to—er—*look*."

Alice gave her eyes another dab, blew her nose and took charge. "Oh, you two soft, sentimental men! Give *me* the plate. I shan't be afraid to open the kennel door. As for the silence, Chubb does appear to be buried several feet down. And he never *was* easy to waken at the best of times. And he probably got hold of some of that ghastly schnapps last night. After all, what with the BBC and the police off duty and practically the entire population of Kent, there wasn't a drop of brandy in the house. However, if the worst comes to the worst, we must just face the facts. He *was* getting on in years."

She held the plate of cold sausages in one hand, dabbed her eyes with the other, and went on, "He will live on in our memories. I, for one, will not forget him. The way he plodded faithfully at my heels, day after day, never taking his eyes off me as I went about my work. The way he looked at you with that dear, doggie gaze. Appealingly, yes, appealingly. The snuffle of his voice, the tread of his quaint feet across a newly polished floor. And the wag of his funny old tail as he collected the nearly empty glasses. It was just as he would have wished, to pass his last hours alone—spared the final ordeal of being harried and kicked by these *awful* Glockensteinians..."

She saved her final sniff for Barney. "I don't see that any of us can be blamed, though it is possible that an unaccustomed diet of sauerkraut and onions dealt the final blow to his digestion!"

Alice had been gone for some time, leaving Mr Peacock and Barney to bite their thumbs and pace the room in suspense, when there was a further visit from Herr Fink.

For some reason his round, worried face looked unexpectedly cheerful and even the familiar twitch was scarcely noticeable. "Ah, Herr Peacock, Herr Stoat. I bring the good news! The Princess Katerina is perfectly safe. Our excellent Gertrude discovered her fast asleep in the pink bedroom. The good surprise—hein? However, as you are aware, Her Highness has a way of, how you put it, scarpering off in search of the adventure. One day, perhaps, in Glockenstein's illustrious future, we shall have the Queen worthy of her crown. Hah! *She* will not be at the beck and call of every cocker-sparrow, but the brave spirit, perhaps, to lead us to victory in battle!"

"Yeah," nodded Barney Stoat. "We had one like that, once. Name of Boadicea. Tore round all over the shop in a chariot."

Mr Peacock rubbed his hands. "Well, well, Herr Fink, we are delighted with the news. It would have been a pity to have spoilt what I trust has not been an entirely inhospitable, or of course, forgettable, stay under the roof of our humble little Highway Inn."

"True, mein Herr. It seems that the snow is melting, and we shall not after all require the landing of the helicopter. We shall make our way, after the excellent lunch which I'm sure Herr Stoat

will provide." Then a new frown appeared over Herr Fink's small nose. "There is—um—just one little favour I would request?"

"Certainly, Herr Fink. Entirely at your service, as always."

"We are having some—er—difficulty in approaching Her Highness's room. The chauffeur, Franz, succeeded eventually in gaining access by means of borrowing a broom from your kitchen."

"A *broom,* Herr Fink?" gasped Mr Peacock.

"It is nothing, nothing," shrugged Herr Fink. "A mere, as you say, inconvenience. Your hound, you understand, which has for some time been ensconced, presumably on guard, outside the Princess

Katerina's door. He is the elderly dog, no? Perhaps he has the bee in the bonnet, and has taken it upon himself to prevent any of my entourage from entering! Herr Peacock, since there are the arrangements to make for our departure, would you be so kind as to go and administer, shall we say, the prod?"

"Great Scott!" gasped Mr Peacock. "Are you telling us that Chubb is *alive*? *And* in possession of his senses?"

Herr Fink twitched just a little. "Alive, mein Herr? There can be little doubt. As for the senses, there may be the difference of opinion! The worthy Gustave who has no difficulty whatsoever in handling our formidable Heinz, was extremely reluctant to make the *second* attempt to reach the Princess despite the fact that he was carrying the brass bed pan at the time—one of the ornaments, I believe, borrowed from your excellent saloon bar."

9

It was not until the evening, when all the tumult had at last died away, that Mr Peacock and Chubb had an opportunity for a chat—to the carefully tuned strains, on the hi-fi, of a march played by the Grenadier Guards.

"Well now, old chap, so it is all over. By now the Princess will be safely on her Royal Yacht, and we are no longer favoured with the immediate attentions of the Kent Constabulary. The BBC, also, have passed on, to film an edition of 'Gardener's World', I believe. I'm sure they will find all those plants most restful after their improvised, and entirely fictitious, attack on Colditz Castle. The papier mâché turrets were washed away in the thaw and I must say the police made a quick and efficient job of rolling up the electric fence. That generator was beginning to make my ears hum and, as far as I can tell, its only effect was to short-circuit the electricity in the saloon bar. All in all, old fellow, you must be sorry to have missed the fun. Not, as it worked out, that there was ever a serious threat to her Royal Highness—nothing, so to speak, to get your teeth into, had you not—ah—been indisposed and unavoidably out of touch."

"Grumph!" said Chubb.

"I do believe your cold has almost cleared up. Perhaps the highly competent Mr Whelp had a point—less food and more fresh air obviously worked wonders."

The Basset Hound wriggled amidst his cushions. "We'll let that pass, Inspector. The question remains, however, whether my survival was the result of a questionable diagnosis and, of far greater significance, a course of treatment so diabolicous that a dog of lesser breed might have succumbed. Particularly having been abandoned under several feet of snow. As to the events under review, Inspector, I will refer to a certain dictum. I remember, in my days at the Yard, one often had recourse to it. As the Commissioner himself once said, concerning the Case of the Five Footed Dray Horse..."

"Yes, yes," said Mr Peacock. "A dictum, Chubb?"

The Basset Hound pushed his nose a little closer into the cushions. "Quite simple, Inspector. One is aware how essential it is to solve a *case*. But what one sometimes overlooks is that it is equally advisable to solve the *no-case*. In short, it was quite obvious from the start that this whole affair was a pink herring, the result, no doubt, of panic in high places."

Mr Peacock shook his head. "Ah, but we did have a scare or two, old chap. I should know. For part of the time I was personally in charge of the investigation. The Superintendent was put out of action, an unprovoked attack, it appears, by a dog or dogs unknown."

At this point Chubb produced a strange throaty sound which might have been caused by the remains of his *Virus Caninculus,* or it might have been merely that he was attempting to hum in tune with the music, or perhaps it was a half stifled chuckle which Mr Peacock thought it best to ignore. "Naturally, I eliminated various suspects one by one—I rather think you would have approved, old chap. Gustave the bodyguard, for instance. No one so obviously villainous could possibly be capable of a crime against the State. Herr Fink was much too nervous and twitchy, Gertrude, the Princess's chaperone inclined to hysteria—she flitted about a lot worrying about the colour of Her Highness's sheets and reducing poor Alice to tears. We did for a time—that is, Barney and I—wonder about the chauffeur, Franz. His request for eggs and chips, then rhubarb tart and custard was, we agreed, a little suspicious."

Chubb yawned. "Suspicious perhaps, Inspector. But rather more, I would say, indiscreet. Surely you know Franz was acting incognito?"

"I don't quite follow, old chap."

"We met on the landing, you know. I had occasion to confiscate his broom. I recognised him at once—a somewhat junior and oafish officer employed on menial duties at the Yard in my time. Something of a dogsbody, in fact. Name of Jones."

"Good gracious!"

"I presume they palmed him off on the Glockenstein Authorities as undercover man, no doubt half hoping he would fall foul of an assassin! Grmph! You were not informed of this? Well, as I well remember, the Glockensteinians are a cautious breed, not inclined to disclose their state secrets to all and sundry."

Something in the Basset Hound's tone irritated Mr Peacock, who resorted to a rare touch of sarcasm. "I am well aware that a Basset Hound, even with a blocked up nose, has a trick or two to teach us stupid humans! On the other hand, certain of your belated activities, old chap, leave much to be desired. Why, may I ask, were you so long about telling us that the Princess Katerina, in the midst of all the hue and cry, was tucked up with you in your kennel?"

"Precautious, Inspector," said Chubb, complacently. "Purely precautious. At that time, you remember, one couldn't be certain this was a *no-case.*" The Basset Hound shifted his large body, flicked his tail and set his still slightly gummy eyes on the Inspector. "Besides which, there were matters of importance to discuss. It is so seldom that one meets Royalty face to face—although, considering the deep gloom to which we were both subjected, it was more a matter of word to word."

"Good lord!" exclaimed Mr Peacock. "Don't tell me, old chap, that you broke the rules? You actually *spoke* to Her Highness?"

"Mere trivialities, Inspector. The Common Market. The policy that Glockenstein is about to adopt towards NATO. Also, a new bill which the Princess will rush through Parliament, the moment she inherits the throne, introducing the severest penalties for those guilty of atrocities against the canine community. However, the Princess shortly fell asleep as I was speaking and I was not about to disturb her when persons came thumping on my door bearing, as my nose told me, plates of congealing sausages."

Mr Peacock sighed with exasperation. "We even sent Alice along, you know. She rather wanted to take a bunch of flowers to lay upon your grave, but Barney and I dissuaded her. It seems that she was half way to your kennel when she spotted you crawling along the fence, alone. Apparently the Dobermann, Heinz, was on the lookout and what did you do, old fellow? Confront the brute, challenge him to a duel, show the flag a bit? Oh, no! According to Alice you deliberately avoided him. And what you thought you were up to, I can't imagine. But for the sudden thaw, and Barney's industry with his spade, both you and the Princess you had just heartlessly abandoned, might have been buried alive."

"*Abandoned* her, Inspector?" snorted the Basset Hound. "Certainly not! It was simply that, having an errand in mind, I dared not approximate myself to the odious Heinz."

"In case he mauled you to pieces, of course!"

"Not at all. He would at once have picked up the scent of the Princess and known that I had harboured her, placing Her Highness under my personal surveillance throughout the night. How was I to tell whether the Dobermann was in league with a possible terrorist? That is why I gave him a wide berth, Inspector. Compared with a Basset Hound, a Dobermann has a poor nose, but even a guinea pig could have sniffed out the truth."

"I see. The plot thickens, old chap! Forgive me for saying so but this errand you mention... it would seem that mischievous young lady had you completely under her thumb. Alice saw you return from your evasive walk with something in your mouth. A lead and collar, no less, since identified as belonging to the police dog, Rex, which you took back to your kennel and laid at those dainty Royal feet. *Why,* old chap? So that she could drag you hither and thither? A trifling disappointment, Chubb. I never thought I would live to see the day when you behaved like a lackey! What happened next? Did the Princess tug you along like a poodle?"

Chubb apparently took all this in good part. There was another of those mysterious chuckles.

"Not at all, Inspector. *I* tugged *her*. I confess that the thought occurred to me that, having fastened Rex's collar about my neck, not too tightly, I am glad to say—I was able to worry if off on completion of my mission—Her Highness might have harboured some childish dream of leading me off to frolic in the snow, but naturally I was having none of it. I tugged her, in the line of duty of course, straight to her pink bedroom. Upon which, having shared my privations of the night, she immediately dropped off to sleep again."

"Ah!" cried Mr Peacock. "And you were cunning enough to watch, out of sight, when the chaperone Gertrude discovered her before taking up your stance on the landing. That was somewhat unnecessary, you know."

"Not at all, Inspector. Unnecessary it was not.

The enemy might still have been in our midst. In fact, I was not at all reassured to the contrary upon being assaulted—three times. Once with a broom, twice with a monstrous brass bed warmer stolen, presumably, from the saloon bar. Humans, I decided, who would attack an old dog in such a despicuous fashion, and before breakfast too, might stop at nothing. Ah—I fear the warming pan has several dents in it, not to mention a row of tooth marks."

"Think nothing of it, old chap," said Mr Peacock. "After all, Alice has her electric blanket back. And I think a new broom can wait a week or two. Well, to coin a phrase, all's well that ends well. I'm rather hoping for a telegram from Glockenstein, upon the safe arrival of the Princess Katerina. One appreciates a little gratitude, don't you agree? A commendation might even enhance the reputation of the Highway Inn—*two* stars, what?"

It was at this point that Mr Peacock noticed, or rather heard, despite the thump-ta-ra of the Grenadier Band, the faintest of tinkling sounds which evidently originated in the region of Chubb's neck.

Possibly the Basset Hound had made a point of shaking his head, rattling the object on something hard.

"I say, what is that round your neck? A purple ribbon, I do declare—something twinkling at the end . . ."

Chubb effected an unusual degree of modesty,

shrugged his huge shoulders and said, "Oh, a mere trinket, Inspector. A decoration, you know. Small token of esteem and recognition—one had, after all, done one's best . . . Her Highness was kind enough to present it to me, with the minimum of ceremonial, before her departure in the Mercedes. Herr Franz, as he calls himself, was busy changing a tyre at the time. The Gold Star of Glockenstein. With Cluster, of course."